SOUND INNOVATIONS

for CONCERT BAND

A Revolutionary Method for Beginning Musicians

Robert **SHELDON** | Peter **BOONSHAFT** | Dave **BLACK** | Bob **PHILLIPS**

Congratulations on deciding to be a member of the band!

This book is here to help you get started on a very exciting time in your life. The audio recordings and DVD will help you practice and develop new skills. When you complete the book, you'll be well prepared to play many types and styles of music. Playing in the band will bring you many years of incredible experiences.

Maybe you'll make music an important part of your life by attending concerts, playing in a community band and supporting the arts. Maybe you'll pursue a career in music as a performer, teacher, composer, sound engineer or conductor. Whatever you choose, we wish you the best of luck in becoming a part of the wonderful world of music!

Practice *Sound Innovations* with SmartMusic® Interactive Software

Transform the way you practice. Instead of practicing alone, you play with background accompaniment and hear how your part fits within the whole. *And,* you get instant feedback. You see which notes you've played right or wrong and hear a recording of your performance.

Try SmartMusic today! Get the first 100 lines of music—free—by downloading SmartMusic at **www.smartmusic.com** to get started. Use code SIBAND when prompted during the activation process.

The MP3 CD includes recorded accompaniments for every line of music in your *Sound Innovations* book. These instrument-specific recordings can be played with the included SI Player, easily uploaded to your MP3 player or transferred to your computer. Additionally, many CD and DVD players are equipped to play MP3s directly from the disc. To play an accompaniment, simply choose the file that corresponds to the line of music in the book. Each line has been numbered and named for easy reference.

Also included on the MP3 CD is the SI Player *with* Tempo Change Technology. The SI Player features the ability to change the speed of the recordings without changing pitch—slow the tempo down for practice or speed it up to performance tempo! Use this program to easily play the included MP3 files or any audio file on your computer.

ISBN-10: 0-7390-6741-9
ISBN-13: 978-0-7390-6741-9

Instrument photos courtesy of Yamaha Corporation of America Band & Orchestral Division

Instrumentation

Teacher's Score	Horn in F
Flute	Trombone
Oboe	Baritone/Euphonium Bass Clef
Bassoon	Baritone/Euphonium Treble Clef
B♭ Clarinet	Tuba
E♭ Alto Clarinet	Electric Bass
B♭ Bass Clarinet	Mallets
E♭ Alto Saxophone	Percussion
B♭ Tenor Saxophone	Combined Percussion
E♭ Baritone Saxophone	Piano Accompaniment
B♭ Trumpet	

About the Authors

Robert Sheldon

Well-known composer/music educator and lead author of *SI for Concert Band*, Robert Sheldon has taught instrumental music in the Florida and Illinois public schools, and has served on the faculty at Florida State Univeristy. As Concert Band Editor for Alfred, he maintains an active composition and conducting schedule, and regularly accepts commissions for new works. An internationally recognized clinician, Sheldon has conducted numerous Regional and All-State Honors Bands throughout the United States and abroad.

Peter Boonshaft

Hailed as one of the most exciting and exhilarating voices in music education today, Peter Boonshaft has been a guest clinician in every state in the U.S., as well as internationally. He is the author of the critically acclaimed books *Teaching Music with Passion*, *Teaching Music with Purpose*, and *Teaching Music with Promise*. Having taught for 29 years, he is currently on the faculty of Hofstra University in Hempstead, New York. Dr. Boonshaft has received honors from political leaders around the world and has been selected three times as a National Endowment for the Arts "Artist in Residence."

Dave Black

A native of Texas, percussionist, and prolific composer Dave Black has been the recipient of many awards and commissions, including 21 consecutive ASCAP Popular Composer Awards and two GRAMMY® participation/nomination certificates. Black is the author or co-author of many best-selling percussion books including the best-selling *Alfred's Drum Method*, Books 1 & 2 and *Alfred's Beginning Drumset Method*. Black is also an active member of the Percussive Arts Society (PAS) and currently serves as Vice President and Editor-in-Chief, School & Church Publishing, for Alfred.

Bob Phillips

Pedagogue, composer, and teacher trainer, Bob Phillips is renowned as a leader in music education and is the lead author of *SI for String Orchestra*. During his 27 years teaching strings and winds in Michigan, Phillips built a thriving orchestra program that was a national model of excellence. A recognized expert in the use of large group pedagogy, he has presented clinics throughout the nation and around the world. Phillips has authored more than 50 books including Alfred's Philharmonic series. His conducting resumé includes professional, all-state, and youth orchestras and he currently serves as Director of String Publications for Alfred and is President-Elect of the American String Teachers Association.

1   **Tuning note for woodwinds, brass and electric bass.**

Level 1: Sound Beginnings

OUR FIRST NOTE—*Introducing the new note, concert D.*

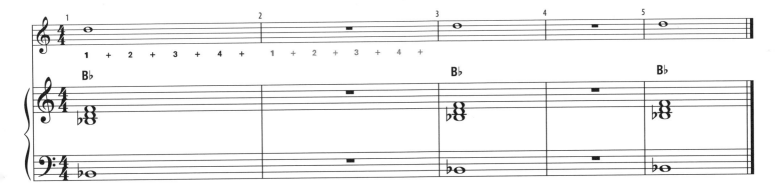

OUR SECOND NOTE—*Introducing the new note, concert C.*

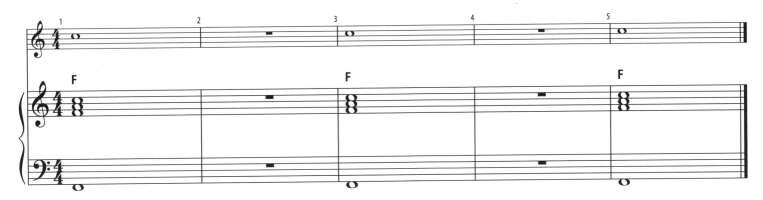

TWO-NOTE TANGO—*Practice going from one note to the other.*

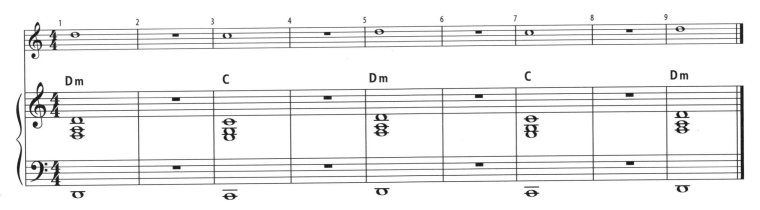

OUR THIRD NOTE—*Introducing the new note, concert Bb.*

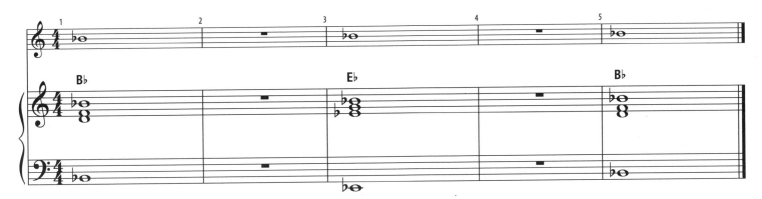

6 **THREE-NOTE COMBO**—*Practice playing all three notes.*

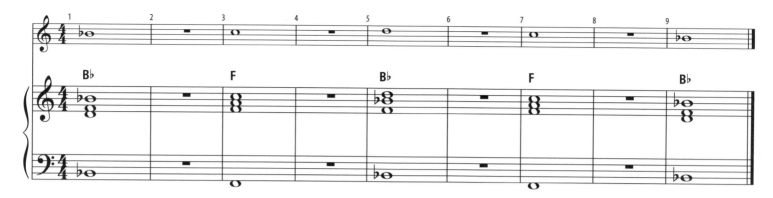

7 **THIRD TIME'S THE CHARM**—*Additional practice on these three notes.*

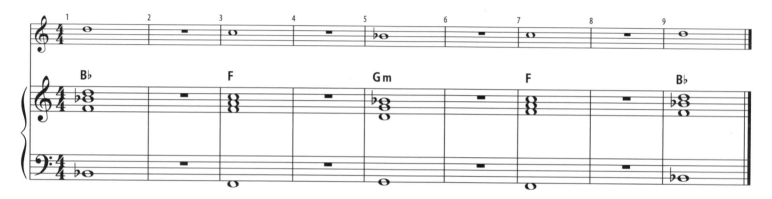

8 **MATCH THE PITCH**—*Play the solo part as the rest of the band answers with the same note. Take turns with other band members.*

9 **A BREATH OF FRESH AIR**—*Name each note before you play.*

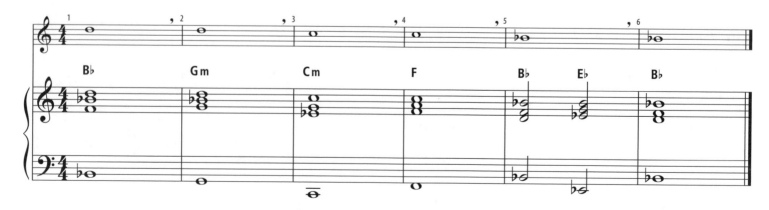

BREATHING EASY—*Sing the notes, then play. For percussionists, clap the rhythms, then play.*

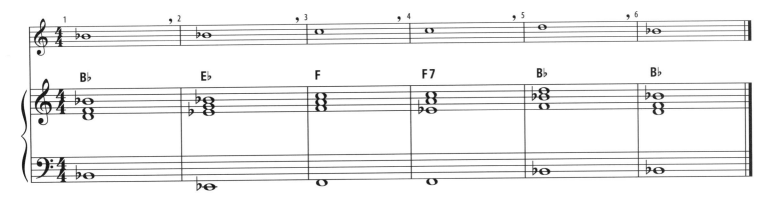

THREE-ZY DOES IT!—*Practice playing three different notes in a row.*

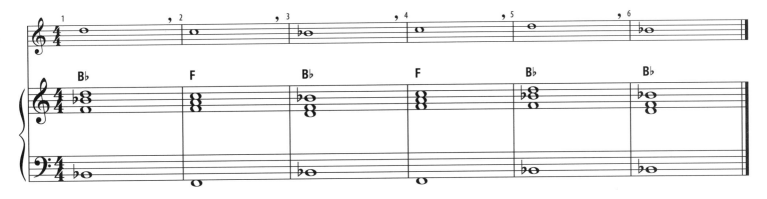

HALF THE TIME—*Introducing half notes and half rests. Repeat as indicated. Clap the rhythm as you count the beats, then sing the piece before you play.*

MIX IT UP—*Play each group of half notes in one breath while changing notes. Electric bass, play each group of half notes using alternating right-hand fingers.*

14 **DUET? DO IT!**—*Introducing our first duet.*

15 **NAME THE NOTES**—*Write the name of each note in the space provided, then sing the notes before you play.*

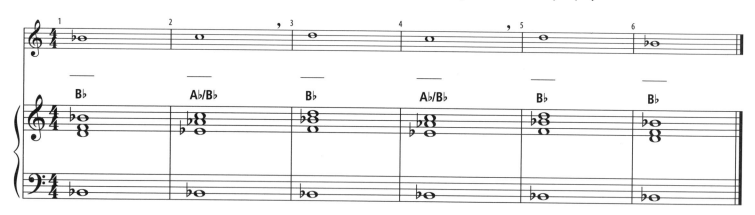

16 **QUARTER NOTES**—*Introducing quarter notes and quarter rests. Play each group of notes in one breath. Count, clap and sing before you play.*

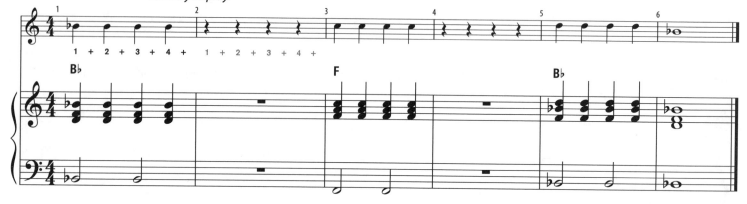

QUARTERLY REPORT—*Name each note before you play.*

HOT CROSS BUNS—*Play the phrase, not just the notes!*

English Folk Song

OUR FOURTH NOTE—*Introducing the new note, concert E♭.*

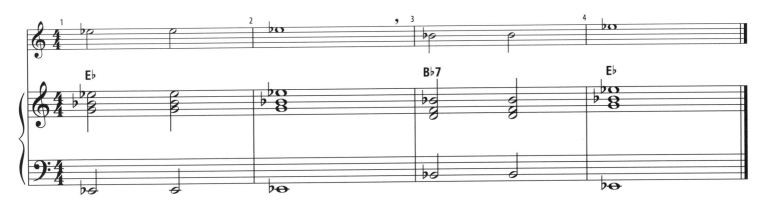

SCALING THE WALL—*Practice using your newest note. Breathe only at the breath marks and rests.*

21 OUR FIFTH NOTE—*Introducing the new note, concert F.*

22 SCALING NEW HEIGHTS—*Practice using another new note.*

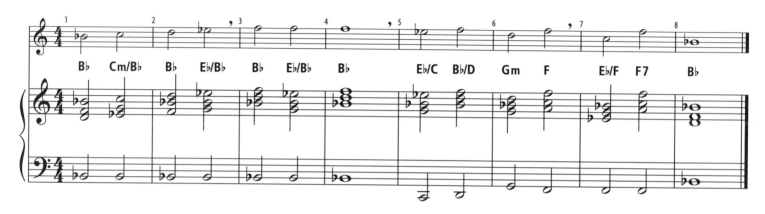

23 MERRILY WE ROLL ALONG—*Breath marks help define the phrases. Electric bass, hold your left-hand finger down through the entire last bar.*

Traditional

24 AU CLAIRE DE LA LUNE—*More phrase and note practice. Add breath marks to create your own musical phrases. Electric bass, play smoothly.*

French Folk Song

25 JINGLE BELLS—*Play this piece in common time and notice the* fermata *at the end. Count, clap and sing before you play.*

James Lord Pierpont

26 GO TELL AUNT RHODY—*More practice in common time with a fermata.*

American Folk Song

27 LIGHTLY ROW—*Play this duet in common time. Switch parts on the repeat.*

Traditional

28 GOOD KING WENCESLAS—*The soloist and full band take turns playing.*

Traditional English Carol

29 SWEETLY SINGS THE DONKEY (round)—*Play this round by having players or groups start every four measures. This piece continues on the next staff, which does not need to show the meter.*

American Folk Song

30 FERMATAS 'R US—*Your teacher will indicate how long to hold each fermata.*

1 **DREYDL, DREYDL**—*Here is a holiday song that uses all the notes you have learned.*

Traditional Hanukkah Song

2 **WARM-UP CHORALE**—*Play with a beautiful sustained tone. Listen for the harmony!*

3 **TIE AND TIE AGAIN**—*Play the tied notes full value. This piece can be played as a duet along with the Warm-Up Chorale.*

Level 2: Sound Fundamentals

34 **OUR SIXTH NOTE**—*Introducing the new note, concert G.*

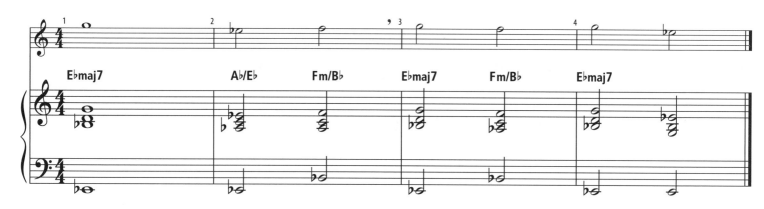

35 **TWINKLING STARS**—*Play this familiar melody using your new note.*

Adapted by Wolfgang Amadeus Mozart

36 **JOLLY OLD ST. NICK**—*Here is a duet that uses your new note.*

Traditional Carol

TWO-FOUR OUT THE DOOR—*This exercise has two beats per measure. Count, clap and sing before you play.*

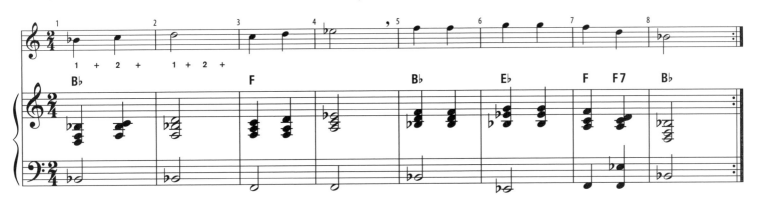

LONDON BRIDGE—*Here's a melody you know in ⅔ time. How many beats does the last note receive?*

English Folk Song

TWO-FOUR OLD MAC—*Name each note before you play.*

Traditional

14

40 **TECHNIQUE BUILDER**—*Practice slowly at first, then gradually get faster each time you play.*

41 **SOUNDS NEW!**—*Introducing the new note, concert A.*

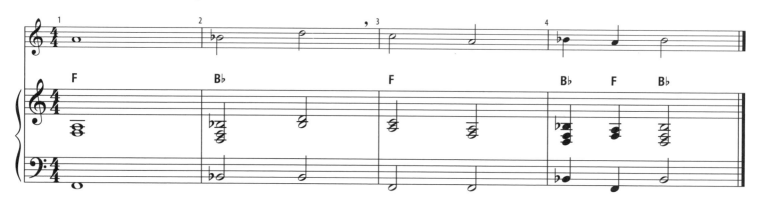

42 **MARY ANN**—*This* calypso *(Caribbean dance) tune uses your new note. Notice the long ties over the bar lines. Discuss with your teacher the characteristics of music in different styles. Listen to the recording of this piece and describe this style of music.*

Caribbean Folk Song

POLLY WOLLY DOODLES—*Take turns conducting the band.*

American Folk Song

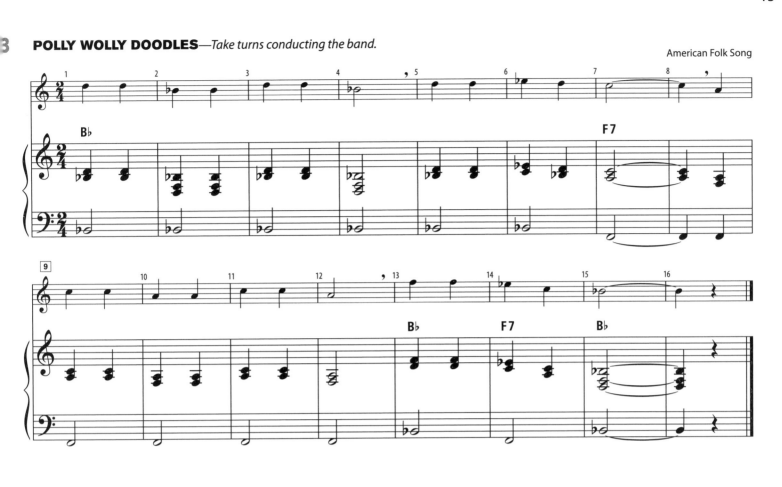

DUET OF THE CRUSADERS

German Folk Song

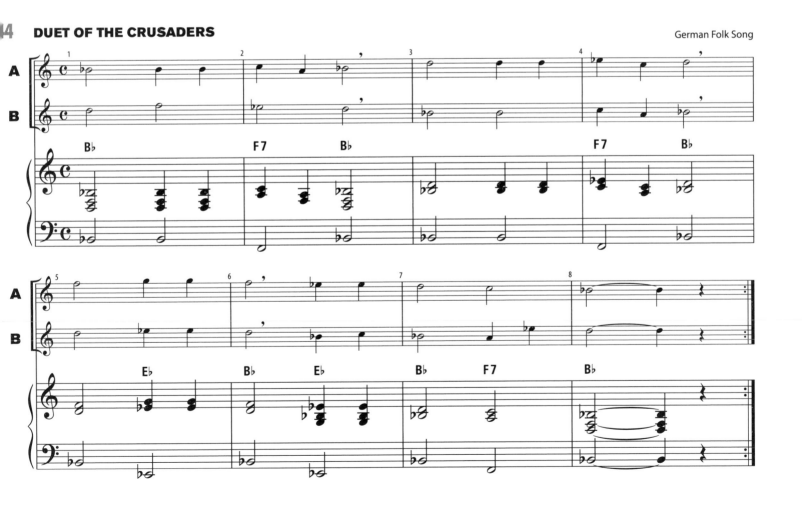

45 **SHOO-FLY!**—*This melody features ties across the bar line.*

American Folk Song

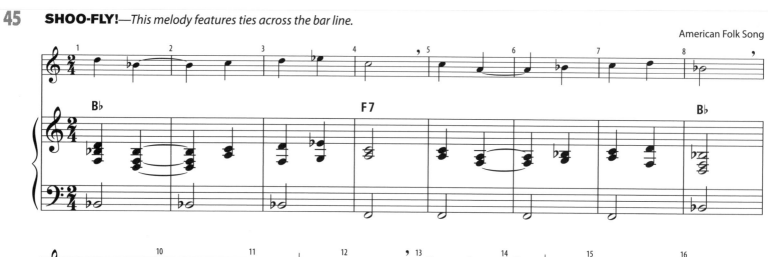

46 **ON THE BRIDGE AT AVIGNON**

French Folk Song

SOUND THEORY—*Draw a clef, meter (hint: look at the last note), bar lines and a final bar line. Write the names of the notes and number of beats for each note before you play.*

* Number of beats: 2 1 1

* Note names: D E♭ E♭

WARM UP—*Play with a beautiful sound and listen to the harmony on the divided notes!*

Gm F B♭ E♭/B♭ B♭ Cm B♭/D F7 Gm E♭ B♭ E♭/B♭ B♭ E♭ B♭/F F F7 B♭

MARCHING MADNESS—*Full band arrangement.*

March tempo (♩ = 120)

F F7 B♭/F F B♭

F7 B♭ F B♭/F F7 B♭

50 **ROCK THIS BAND!**—*Full band arrangement.*

51 **RHYTHM ROUND-UP**—*Clap the rhythm as you count the beats.*

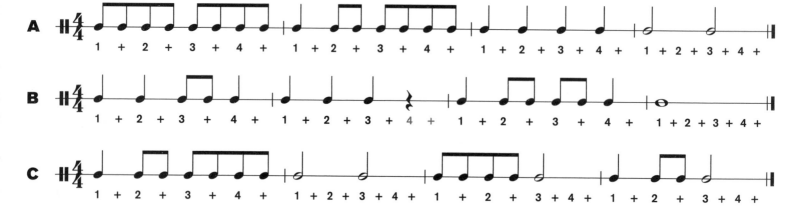

52 **GOTTA HAND IT TO YA! (Clapping Duet)**—*Clap either Part A or B, then switch parts on the repeat.*

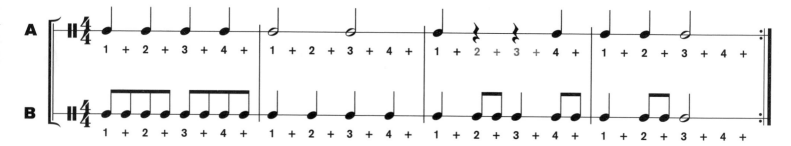

PIECES OF EIGHT—*Count the rhythm first, clap, then play.*

WHISPER AND SHOUT!—*Play the notes with the dynamics indicated.*

55 **LONG, LONG AGO**—*Play this familiar melody with dynamics.*

Thomas Haynes Bayly

56 **SKIP TO MY LOU**—*More fun with dynamics! Name each note before you play.*

American Folk Song

7 DYNAMIC DUET—*Read the dynamics carefully as they are different in each part. Switch parts on the repeat.*

8 THIS OLD MAN—*Here is a tune to play just for fun!*

American Folk Song

59 **SOUNDS NEW!**—*Introducing the new note, concert G.*

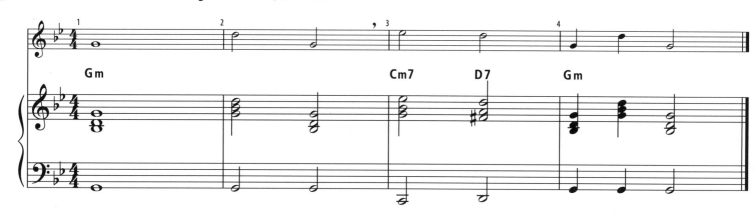

60 **INTERESTING INTERVALS**—*Build your technique. Write the name of each interval in the space provided before you play.*

Interval: 2nd

61 **HEY, HO! NOBODY'S HOME**—*Practice dynamics.*

English Folk Song

62 TURN THE VOLUME UP—*Increase your airstream to create a louder sound. Electric bass, play with more force in your right hand.*

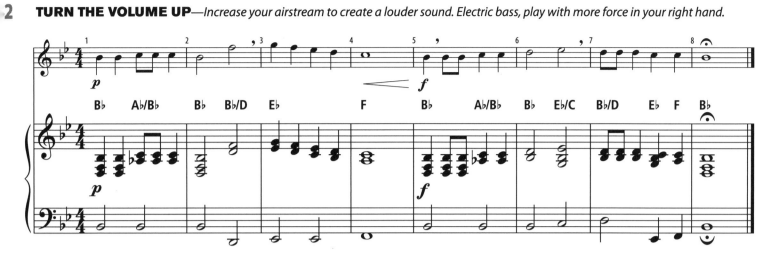

63 TURN THE VOLUME DOWN—*Reduce your airstream to create a softer sound. For extra fun, play this with Turn the Volume Up as a duet. Electric bass, play with less force in your right hand.*

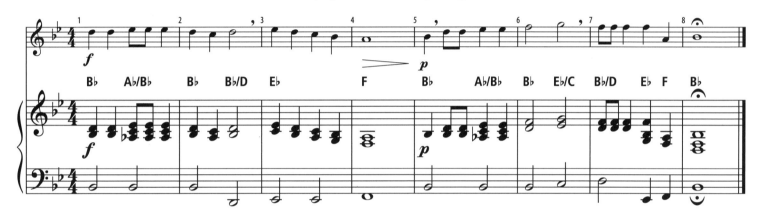

64 FRÈRE JACQUES (round)—*Practice the slurs in this familiar melody (electric bass, play smoothly), then play it as a round.*

French Folk Song

65 A TISKET, A TASKET

American Folk Song

66 JASMINE FLOWER—*Practice the notes and skills you have learned.*

Chinese Folk Song

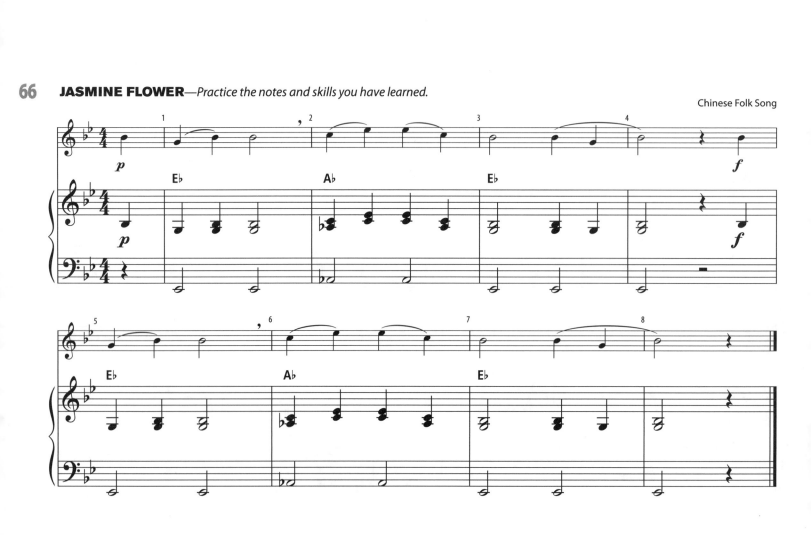

47 **ERIE CANAL**—*How many beats are in the pickup? How many beats are missing from the last measure?*

Thomas S. Allen

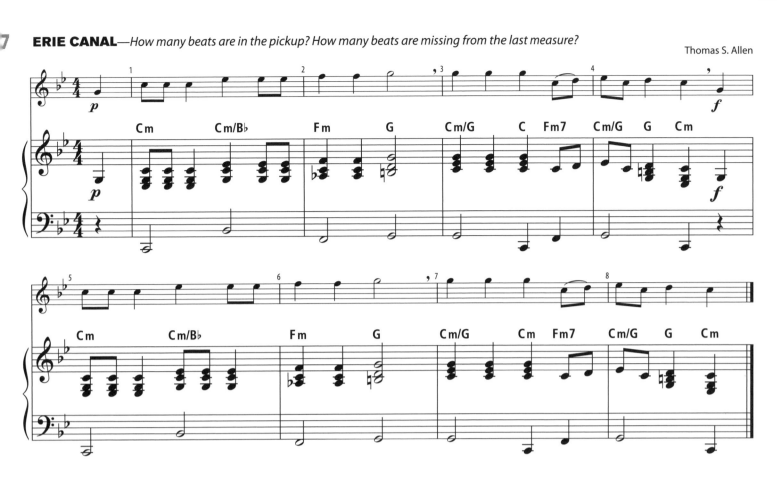

48 **OH! SUSANNAH**

Stephen Foster

69 **THEME AND VARIATIONS ON BLACK SHEEP**—*How does Variation I differ from the Theme?*
How does Variation II differ from the Theme?

English Folk Song

70 **THEME AND VARIATIONS YOUR WAY**—*Write your own variation by changing the rhythm and/or notes, then play it!*

1 **SERENADE**—*Full band arrangement.*

Wolfgang Amadeus Mozart

2 **INVADERS!**—*Full band arrangement. Remember, in $\frac{2}{4}$ time a whole measure rest receives two beats.*

73 **ACADEMIC FESTIVAL OVERTURE**—*Full band arrangement.*

Johannes Brahms

74 **STODOLA PUMPA**—*Practice good posture and breathing skills.*

Czech Folk Song

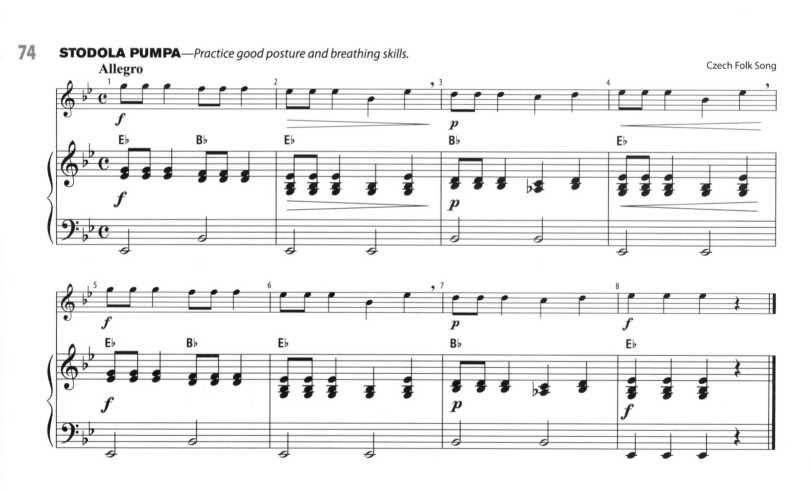

DYNAMITE DYNAMICS—*Review all four of the dynamics you've learned, along with* crescendo *and* decrescendo.

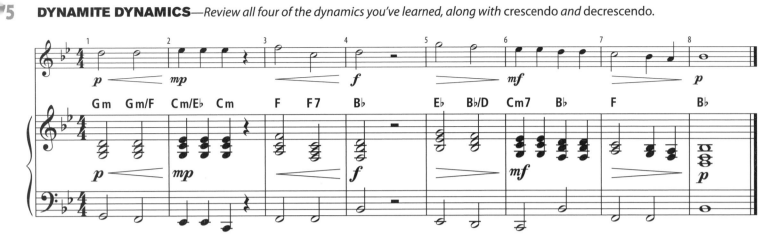

MY OLD KENTUCKY HOME

Stephen Foster

Level 2: Sound Musicianship

77 **SOUNDS NEW!**—*Introducing the new note, concert A♭.*

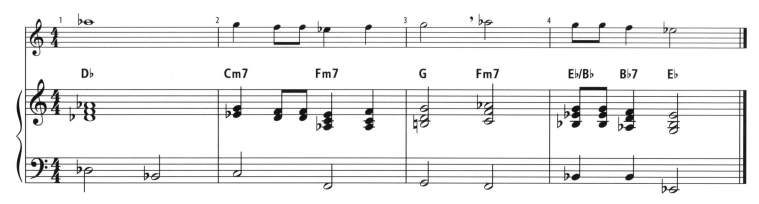

78 **WAY UP HIGH**

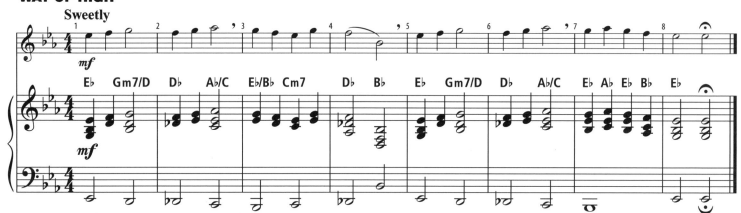

79 **BINGO**—*Before playing, discuss ways in which you can make this sound "light." Name the key.*

American Folk Song

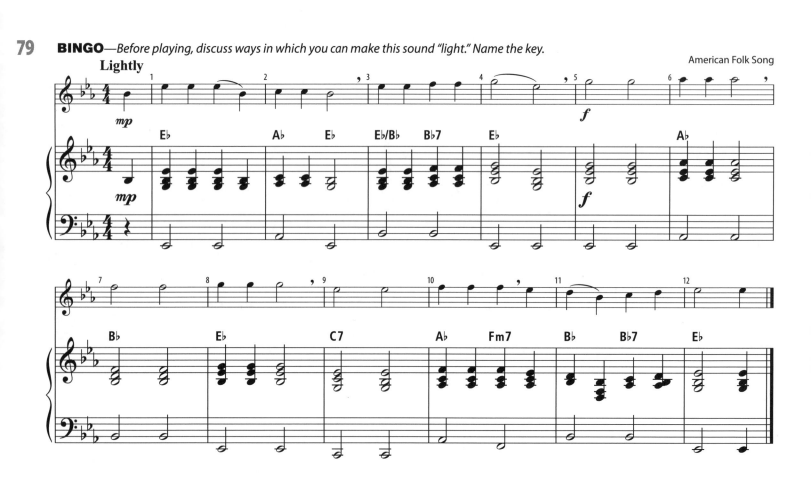

30 **BUFFALO GALS**—*Since this is played with spirit, the tempo should be energetic. Watch the 1st and 2nd endings.*

American Traditional

31 **MUSETTE**—*Here is a tune to play just for fun!*

Johann Sebastian Bach

32 **MEXICAN HAT DANCE**—*Write the number of each beat you play in the space provided. Count, clap and sing before you play. See how well your performance of Mexican Hat Dance captures the style of a dance.*

Mexican Folk Song

83 BARCAROLLE—*Name the key. Look for the breath marks to help you phrase and play this in a gentle style.*
Try memorizing this melody and playing it expressively.

Jacques Offenbach

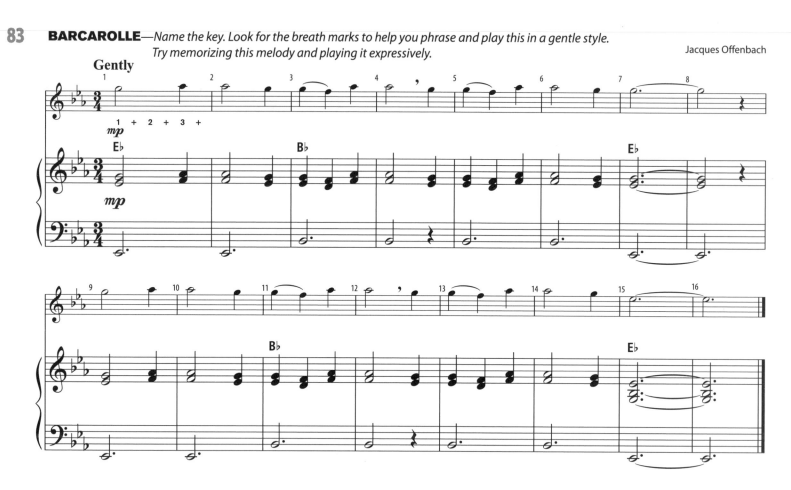

84 MORNING—*Before you play, sing and conduct the following piece. Moderato is a medium tempo.*

Edvard Grieg

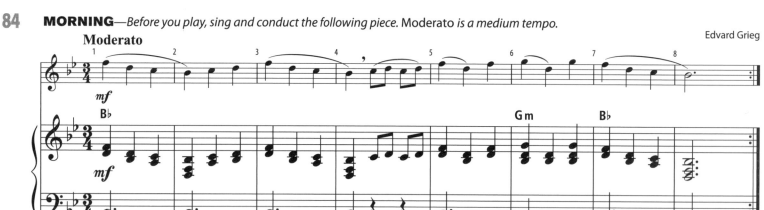

85 SOUNDS NEW!—*Introducing the new note, concert A♭.*

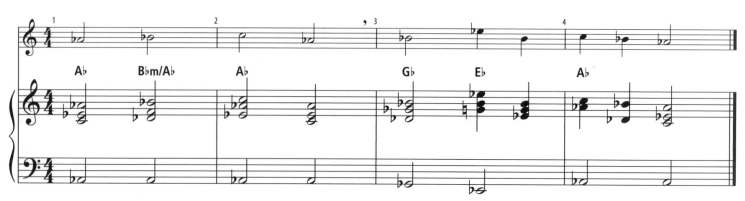

TWO-NOTE TREAT

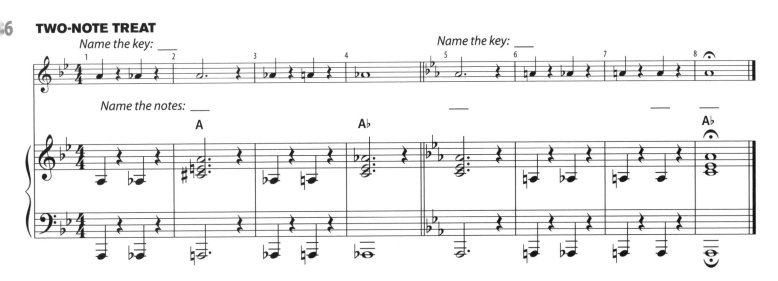

TRAP-EAZY DOES IT!—*Before you play, think about the repeats.*

Gaston Lyle

SOUNDS NEW!—*Introducing the new note, concert F (flute, oboe, clarinet, bass clarinet, alto sax, baritone sax and horn); concert A and B♭ (bassoon, alto clarinet, tenor sax, trumpet, trombone, baritone, tuba, electric bass and mallets).*

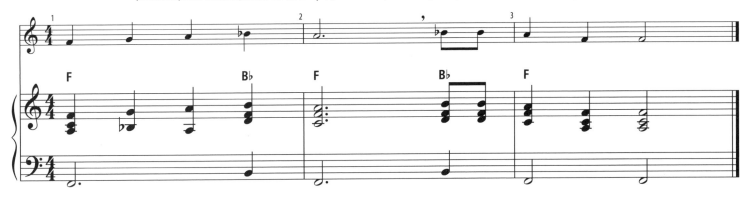

89 **TAKE NOTE**—*What does Largo mean?*

90 **THE CARNIVAL OF VENICE**—*Here is another melody with a pickup note and 1st and 2nd endings.*

Italian Folk Song

91 **CHESTER**—*Chester was often referred to as the "unofficial anthem" of the American Revolution.*

William Billings

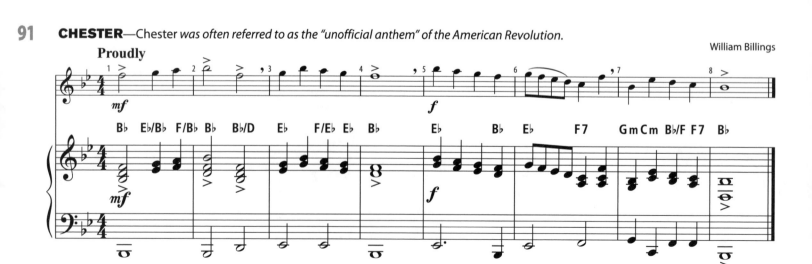

2 MARCHING ALONG—*Circle the accents and the one-measure repeat before you play.*

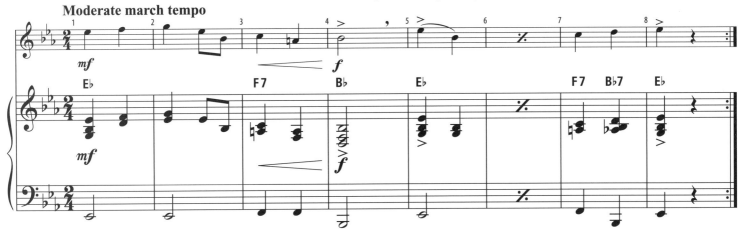

93 EXERCISES ON EIGHTHS—*Demonstrate your understanding of eighth notes and rests by clapping these exercises.*
Switch parts on the repeat.

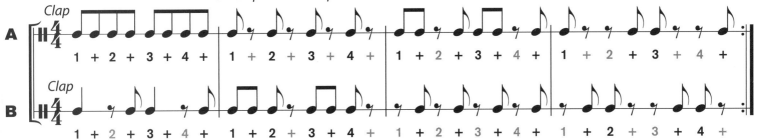

94 EMPHASIS ON ACCENTS—*Try both parts of this clapping duet and be sure to clap louder on the accented notes.*
Before you play, circle the single eighth notes and eighth rests in Part B.

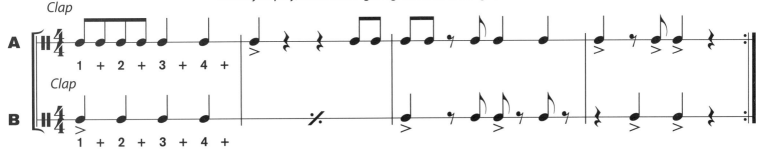

95 EMPHASIS ON NOTES—*Now play the accents by using more air to make the accented notes louder.*
Electric bass, play the accents by using more force in your right hand.

36

96 DOWN BY THE STATION—*Practice eighth notes, slurs and accents.*

American Folk Song

97 BROTHER JOHN (round)

French Folk Song

98 SOUNDS NEW!—*Introducing the new note, concert E.*

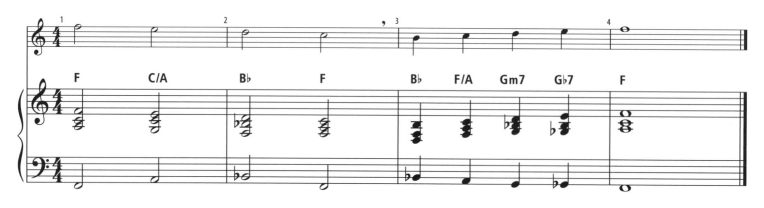

99 AURA LEE—*How does this new key signature affect the notes you will play?*

George R. Poulton

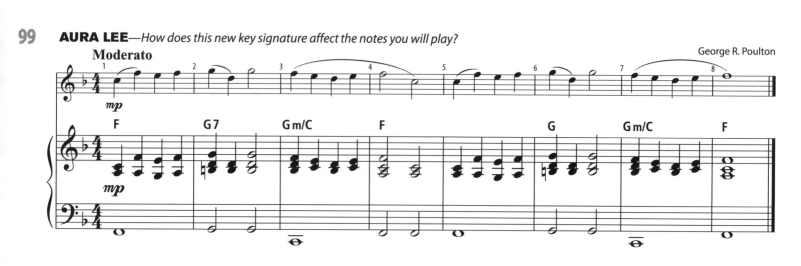

SAKURA—*This melody has a right-facing repeat. Before you play, trace your finger over the "roadmap" of the piece.*

Japanese Folk Song

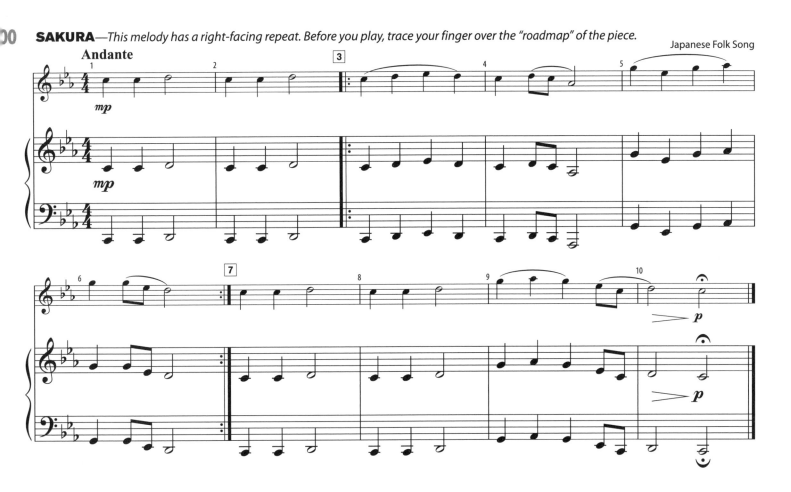

SHE WORE A YELLOW RIBBON—*Here's a tune to play just for fun!*

George A. Norton

102   **A WHOLE LOTTA TIES**—*Feel the pulse of the beat on the tied eighth note.*

103   **A WHOLE LOTTA DOTS**—*Feel the pulse of the beat on the dot.*

104   **THEME FROM THE "NEW WORLD SYMPHONY"**—*Play the D.C., then end at the* Fine.

Antonín Dvořák

95 **JOY TO THE WORLD**—*Full band arrangement.*

Christmas Carol

106 **ACCIDENTAL ENCOUNTERS**—*Before you play, name all the notes.*

107 **ODE TO JOY**—Maestoso *means to play majestically. Circle the "sign" then clap, count and sing before you play.*

Ludwig van Beethoven

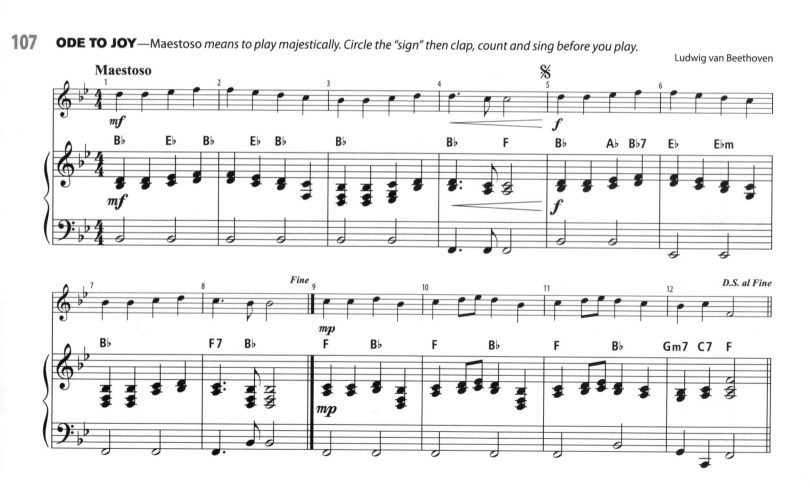

08 AULD LANG SYNE—*Full band arrangement. Circle the multiple-measure rests before you play.*

Scottish Folk Song

09 MICHAEL, ROW THE BOAT ASHORE—*Always play with a beautiful sound.*

African-American Spiritual

Level 4: Sound Development

110 **CONCERT B♭ SCALE**—*Memorize this scale!*

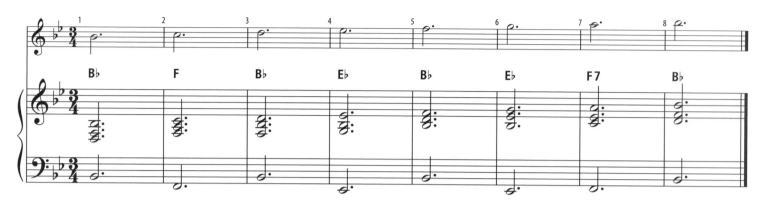

111 **THREE-FOUR, PHRASE SOME MORE**—*This melody starts with a phrase that sounds as if it asks a question, followed by a phrase that sounds as if it provides the answer. Play this as a duet with the Concert B♭ scale.*

112 **DOWN THE ROAD**—*Play with a steady stream of fast air. For electric bass, play with a steady amount of force in your right hand.*

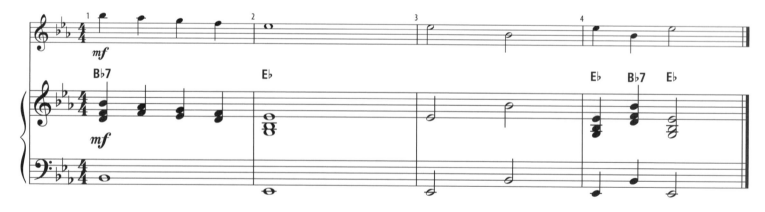

113 **SUO GAN**—*Play this melody in the style of a lullaby.*

Welsh Folk Song

14 **ARTICULATION STATION**—*Play the notes with the indicated articulation.*

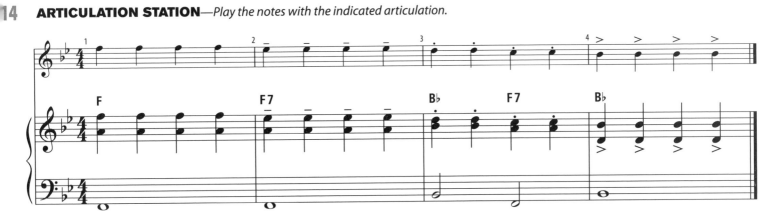

15 **OVERTURE TO "WILLIAM TELL"**—*Here is a familiar tune that uses* legato *and* staccato.

Gioacchino Rossini

16 **SOUNDS NEW!**—*Introducing the new note, concert D♭.*

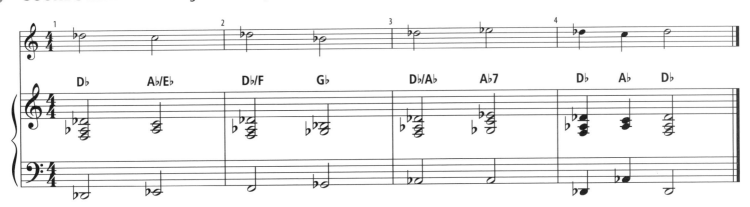

117 **ALGERIAN DANCE**—*Try out your new note on this exotic melody.*

Arabic Folk Song

118 **THE LONG AND SHORT, COMMON TIME, ACCIDENTAL BLUES**—*Try out your new articulation skills! The blues is a type of American music derived from spirituals and work songs.*

119 **ON TOP OF OLD SMOKEY**—*Before you play, look at your key signature and circle all the notes that will be affected. Notice the length of the tied notes.*

American Folk Song

LONG AND SHORT ACCIDENTAL ENCOUNTERS—*Before you play, name all the notes. Watch out for the key change!*
Try this as a duet with the Long and Short, Common Time, Accidental Blues.

GOOD NIGHT LADIES

Traditional

CHROMATIC MARCH—*Try out your half-stepping skills! Find the courtesy accidental.* Alla marcia *tells us to play in the style of a march.*

123 **JAZZ DOO-ETTE**—*Play this piece in the style of the "jazz big bands" popular in the 1930s and 1940s. Name the key.*

124 **ON YOUR OWN!**—*Play the first four measures, then write the last four measures yourself! Now, play the entire piece.*

125 **CAN-CAN**—*Vivo means lively and spirited!*

Jacques Offenbach

26 VOLGA BOAT SONG—Pesante *means to play in a heavy style. Memorize this piece and play in an expressive manner.*

Russian Folk Song

27 ALL THROUGH THE NIGHT—*Name the key.*

Welsh Folk Song

28 ARIRANG—*Name the key. Discuss with your teacher the characteristics of music from different cultures. Listen to the recording of this piece and describe those characteristics.*

Korean Folk Song

48

129 **MINUET**—*A minuet is a French country dance.*

Johann Sebastian Bach

130 **SAILOR'S CHANTEY**—*Name the key.*

Sea Chantey

131 **THEME FROM SWAN LAKE**—*Always play with expression.*

Pyotr Il'yich Tchaikovsky

MAJOR MACARONI (YANKEE DOODLE)—*This is in a major key. How does this make you feel?*

American Traditional

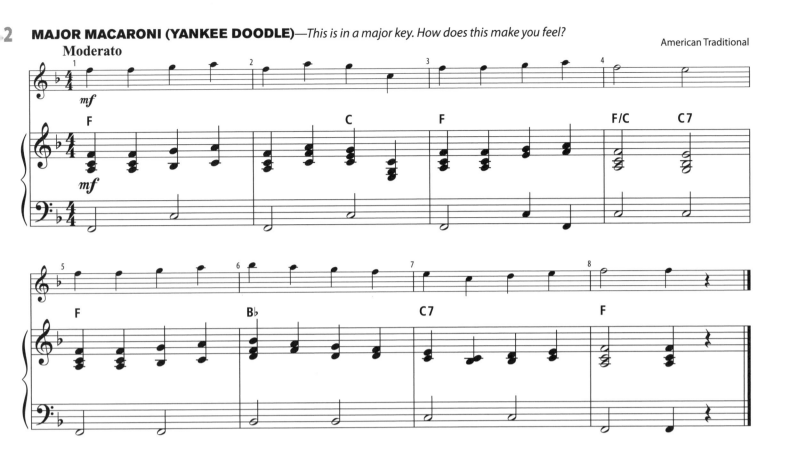

MINOR MACARONI—*This is in a minor key. How does this make you feel? How is it different from* Major Macaroni?

134 **ALOUETTE**—*Is this in a major or minor key?*

Level 5: Sound Technique

37 **RANGE ROVER 1**—*Introducing the new note, concert D (clarinet, alto clarinet, bass clarinet, tenor sax, horn and mallets).*

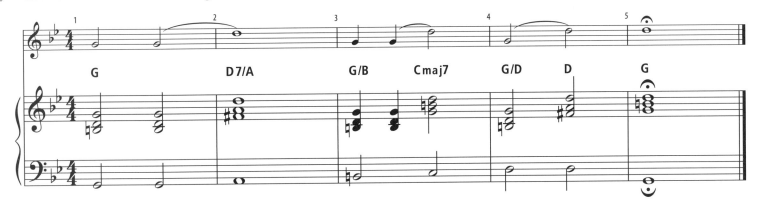

38 **IMPERATIVE INTERLUDE 1**

39 **RANGE ROVER 2**—*Introducing the new note, concert E♭ (clarinet, alto clarinet, bass clarinet and mallets).*

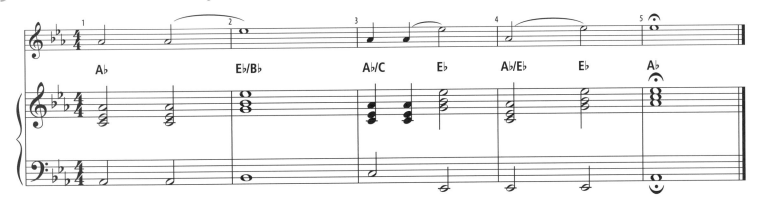

40 **RANGE ROVER 2**

141 **RANGE ROVER 3**

142 **IMPERATIVE INTERLUDE 3**

143 **HIGH FLYING**—*Here's a tune to play just for fun!*

44 RANGE ROVER 4—*Introducing the new note, concert C (flute, oboe, clarinet, alto clarinet, bass clarinet, alto sax, tenor sax, baritone sax and mallets).*

45 IMPERATIVE INTERLUDE 4

46 RANGE ROVER 5

47 IMPERATIVE INTERLUDE 5

148 **RANGE ROVER 6**—*Introducing the new note, concert E (clarinet, alto clarinet, bass clarinet, tenor sax, horn and mallets).*

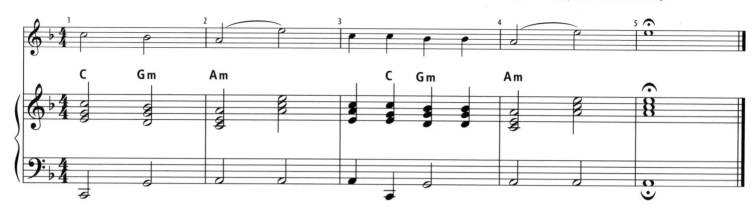

149 **IMPERATIVE INTERLUDE 6**

150 **DRINK TO ME ONLY WITH THINE EYES**—*Practice your slurs with this familiar tune. For electric bass, practice playing smoothly.*

Traditional English Song

61 **IT'S RAINING, IT'S POURING**—*Play this familiar melody with a beautiful sound.*

English Folk Song

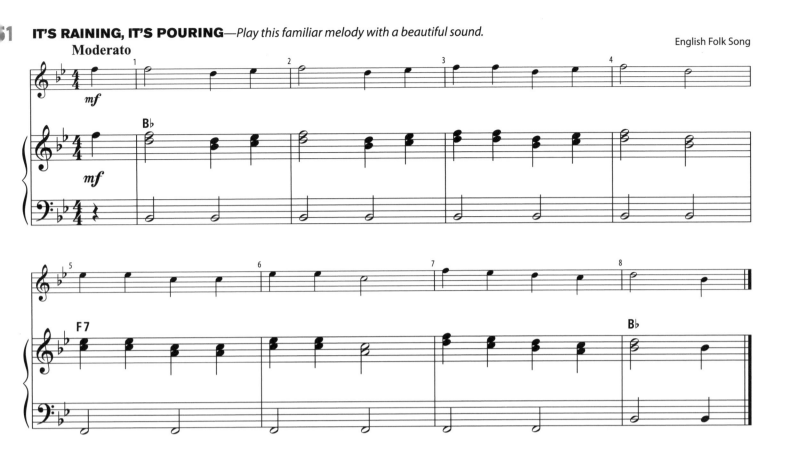

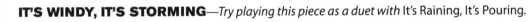

62 **IT'S WINDY, IT'S STORMING**—*Try playing this piece as a duet with* It's Raining, It's Pouring.

153 **RANGE RIDER**—*Introducing the new note, concert D (clarinet, bass clarinet); concert G and A (alto clarinet).*

154 **CRAZY FINGERS**

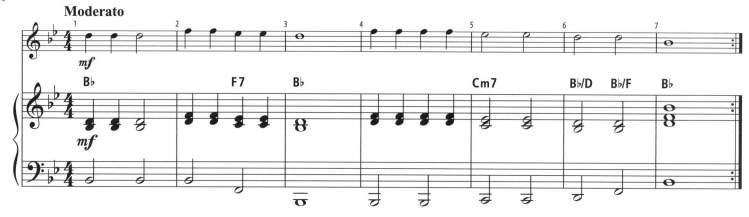

155 **RANGE ROVER 7**—*Introducing the new note, concert A (clarinet and bass clarinet).*

156 **IMPERATIVE INTERLUDE 7**

57 **SWORD DANCE**—*Here's a tune to play just for fun!*

Traditional

58 **BREAK UP**—*Play the phrase, not just the notes. Introducing the new note, concert C (bassoon, baritone B.C., electric bass, trumpet, baritone T.C., trombone and tuba).*

59 **BREAK DOWN**—*Play with a steady stream of fast air. Electric bass, play with a steady amount of force in your right hand.*

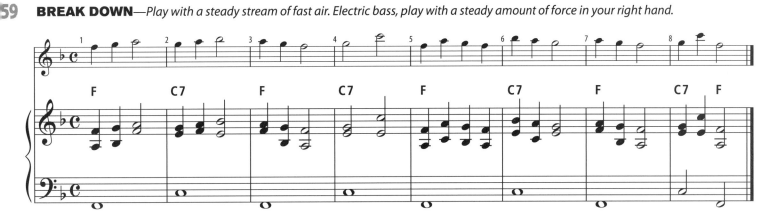

60 **DOWN AND OUT**—*Play with a full sound. For clarinet, alto clarinet and bass clarinet, this exercise crosses the break between registers moving down stepwise from higher notes.*

58

161 **UP AND OVER**—*Demonstrate good posture. For clarinet, alto clarinet and bass clarinet, this exercise crosses the break between registers moving up stepwise from lower notes.*

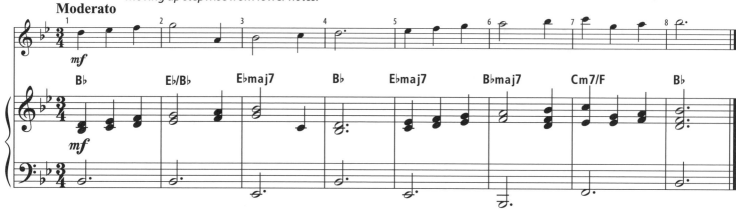

162 **THE CONCERT B♭ MAJOR SCALE**—*Memorize the following ascending and descending scale.*

163 **COUNTRY GARDENS**—*Name the key. Before you play, notice how loud the crescendo becomes.*

English Folk Song

64 CAMPTOWN RACES—*Before you play, notice how soft or loud each dynamic change becomes.*

Stephen Foster

65 WHEN THE SAINTS GO MARCHING IN—*Full band arrangement.*

American Gospel Hymn

166 **SURPRISE SYMPHONY**—*This piece includes a "surprise" created by dynamics. Can you find the big surprise? Discuss with your teacher the characteristics of music written during this period. Listen to the recording of this piece and describe those characteristics.*

Franz Joseph Haydn

167 **HALF-STEP HASSLE**—*Practice your chromatic skills.*

68 HILARIOUS HALF STEPS—*Here is another chromatic challenge. Name the notes before you play.*

69 SYMPHONIC THEME FROM SYMPHONY NO. 1—*Is this a major or minor key?*

Gustav Mahler

70 ETUDE—*This exercise helps you become more comfortable with your chromatic notes.*

171 **CHORALE**—*Full band arrangement. Is this a major or minor key?*

Johann Sebastian Bach

172 **THE GREAT GATE OF KIEV**—*Full band arrangement.* Pictures at an Exhibition *represents a tour through an art gallery. In addition to form and color, music uses many of the same concepts as the visual arts.*

Modest Mussorgsky

Level 6: Sound Performance

73

SOLO: SCARBOROUGH FAIR—*This solo has a piano accompaniment.*

Traditional English Ballad

174 **THE BLUE-TAIL FLY (duet)**

American Minstrel Song

175 **MOLLY MALONE (trio)**—*Learn all three parts.*

Traditional Irish Ballad

76 **TIME TRIALS**—*Count and clap this exercise before you play. This piece reviews all the meters you have learned.*

77 **NEW NAMES FOR OLD FRIENDS**—*Use your knowledge of enharmonics to play this exercise.*

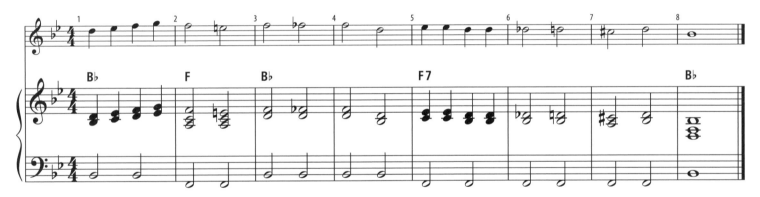

78 **MUSIC MASQUERADE**—*Use your new notes and knowledge of accidentals to play this enharmonic exercise.*

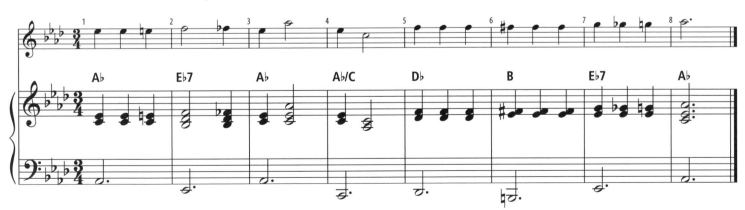

179 **CHROMATIC SCALE**—*This scale includes only half steps and is written with sharps ascending and flats descending.*
After you learn both lines, try playing as a duet.

180 **HABAÑERA**—*This popular operatic melody uses lots of chromatic notes.*

Georges Bizet

1 O CANADA—*This is the Canadian National Anthem. Play this in four-measure phrases by breathing after the long notes.*

Calixa Lavallée

182 **GRANT US PEACE (round)**—*Play this well-known round with the full band or as a trio.*

Traditional

TAKE A RIDE ON THE BLUES TRAIN—*Full band arrangement. Choose from the notes provided and make up a part as you play. This is called* **IMPROVISATION**. *Your director will indicate when it is your turn to improvise.*

184 **SCALE & ARPEGGIO (Key of F Major)**

185 **CHORALE IN CONCERT F MAJOR**—*Full band arrangement.*

186 **SCALE ETUDE (Key of F Major)**

187 **INTERVAL ETUDE (Key of F Major)**

88 SCALE & ARPEGGIO (Key of B♭ Major)

89 CHORALE IN CONCERT B♭ MAJOR—*Full band arrangement.*

90 SCALE ETUDE (Key of B♭ Major)

91 INTERVAL ETUDE (Key of B♭ Major)

192 SCALE & ARPEGGIO (Key of E♭ Major)

193 CHORALE IN CONCERT E♭ MAJOR—*Full band arrangement.*

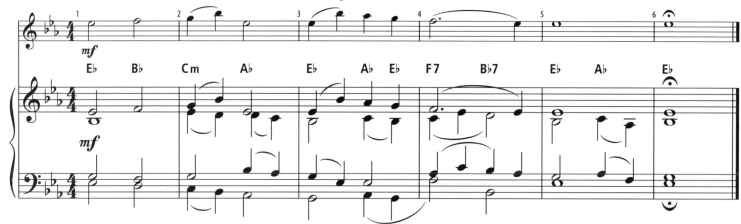

194 SCALE ETUDE (Key of E♭ Major)

195 INTERVAL ETUDE (Key of E♭ Major)

6 **SCALE & ARPEGGIO (Key of A♭ Major)**

7 **CHORALE IN CONCERT A♭ MAJOR**—*Full band arrangement.*

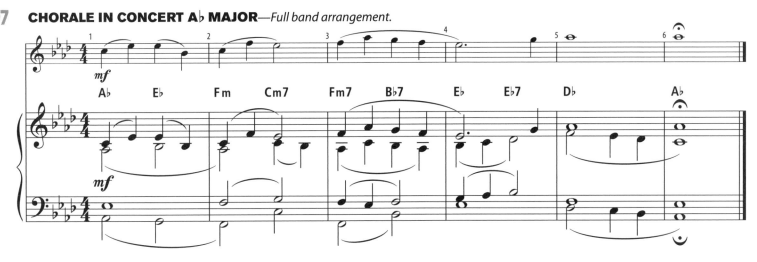

8 **SCALE ETUDE (Key of A♭ Major)**

9 **INTERVAL ETUDE (Key of A♭ Major)**

74

200 **ETUDE #1**

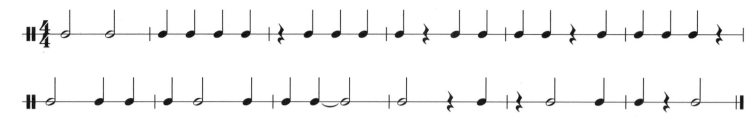

201 **ETUDE #2**

202 **ETUDE #3**

203 **ETUDE #4**

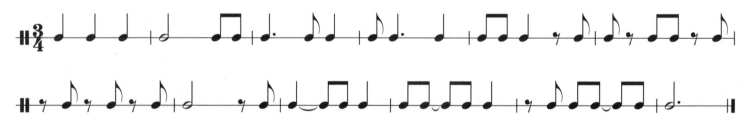

204 **ETUDE #5**